GOOD NEWS!

A BIBLE STUDY & ACTIVITY BOOK
TO EXPLAIN THE GOSPEL

Dear Parent/Teacher,

This activity book is designed to help your child discover and understand the truth in God's Word on their own. **However, they will more than likely need help from you to get started and to help them process what they are reading in the Bible.**

Consider being "nearby" as they work through the activity pages. After they are done, have them show you what they did and ask them questions to increase understanding.

You don't have to do a certain amount of pages on a certain day, but please work your way through this book in order from beginning to end.

The starting point of this activity book is Mark 16:15-16. Your child will learn:
- What is the Good News?
- What does God tell me to believe?
- Why should I be baptized?
- What does it mean to be saved?
- What is condemnation?
- Now that I know about the Good News, tell others!

I pray that this Bible activity book encourages your child to love and know the Lord and His Word.

♡ Heather @ Digging Into God

IMPORTANT

please read!

You have a Heavenly Father who adores you and wants to speak to you! He has GOOD NEWS to tell you and He wants you to understand what that Good News means to you.

God has created you, and He really wants to be friends with you. In fact, He sent His one and only Son--Jesus--to Earth in order to make that happen!

This Bible activity book will help you discover how to be friends with God. **This book is designed for you to start at the beginning, and move your way through it in order.**

God doesn't want you to just say you believe in Him because that is what you're "supposed to" do. He wants you to personally know and understand Him. God tells us what He is like in the Bible, and He allows us to make our own decision as to whether or not we want to be close to Him.

P.S. All Scripture was taken from the New Living Translation Bible (NLT). The "fill in the blanks" throughout this devotional will make more sense if you are able to use that Bible version.

"Go into all the world and preach the

_____ _____

to everyone. Anyone who _____ and is _____ will be _____. But anyone who _____ to believe will be _____."

MARK 16:15-16 (NLT)

GOOD NEWS

"Go into all the world and preach the GOOD NEWS to everyone."
Mark 1:15

WHAT IS THE

GOOD NEWS!?

"THIS IS THE GOOD NEWS ABOUT JESUS THE MESSIAH, THE SON OF GOD."

MARK 1:1

 **FiRST,** let's see if you even need to hear about the Good News. Answer "yes" or "no" to each question:

YES/NO

Have you ever lied? ☐☐

Have you ever been disrespectful to your mom or dad? ☐☐

Have you ever stolen something (big or little)? ☐☐

Have you ever loved something more than you love God? ☐☐

Have you spoken about God in a careless way? ☐☐

Do you believe you are a good enough person and deserve to go to Heaven? ☐☐

If you answered "yes" to any of these questions, it means that you DO need to know about God's Good News. Because if you answered "yes" to any of these questions, it means that you have broken God's Law--you have sinned, and deserve punishment.

(You can read about God's Law in Exodus 20:3-17.)

To put it very simply, we are guilty of turning against God & breaking His Law.

The punishment is death and separation from God for eternity.

 **The Good News is that when Jesus died on the cross, He took care of the punishment we deserved, so we can be close to God again.**

ROMANS 1:16:

FOR I AM NOT ASHAMED OF THIS _____ _____ ABOUT _____.
IT IS THE _____ OF GOD AT WORK, _____ EVERYONE WHO _____.

READ ROMANS 1:16-17

WHO IS THE GOOD NEWS ABOUT?

_____

READ ROMANS 1:17:

THE GOOD NEWS TELLS US HOW GOD MAKES US RIGHT IN HIS SIGHT. HOW DO WE BECOME "RIGHT WITH GOD"?

WHAT DOES IT MEAN TO BE RIGHT WITH GOD?

_____

_____

_____

Make a "word picture" from the following verse
(example: 👁 🖤 U = I love you)

"We are made right with God
by placing our faith in
Jesus Christ. And this is
true for everyone who believes,
no matter who you are."
Romans 3:22

SOLVE THIS CRYPTOGRAM

A cryptogram is a puzzle where each letter in a message is swapped with another letter. To solve it, try to figure out which letters stand for each other to reveal the hidden message—it's a fun code-breaking challenge!

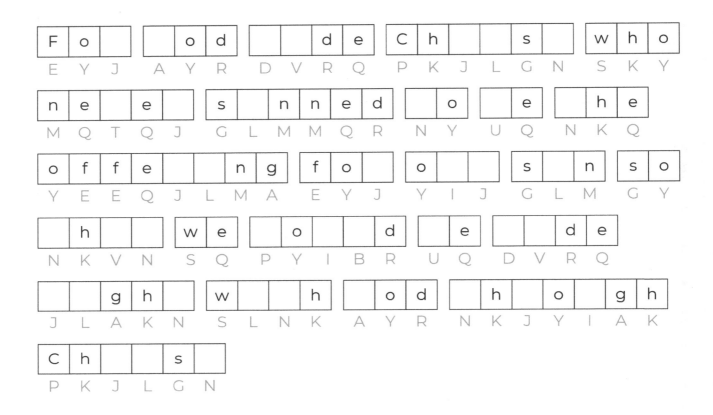

F	o				o	d			d	e	C	h			s		w	h	o
E	Y	J		A	Y	R		D	V	R	Q	P	K	J	L	G	N	S	K	Y

n	e		e		s	n	n	e	d		o		e		h	e
M	Q	T	Q	J		G	L	M	M	Q	R		N	Y		U	Q	N	K	Q

o	f	f	e		n	g	f	o		o			s	n	s	o
Y	E	E	Q	J	L	M	A	E	Y	J		Y	I	J		G	L	M	G	Y

	h		w	e		o		d		e			d	e
N	K	V	N		S	Q	P	Y	I	B	R		U	Q		D	V	R	Q

	g	h		w		h		o	d		h		o		g	h
J	L	A	K	N		S	L	N	K		A	Y	R		N	K	J	Y	I	A	K

C	h			s
P	K	J	L	G	N

→ For the solution, turn to 2 Corinthians 5:21 (NLT)

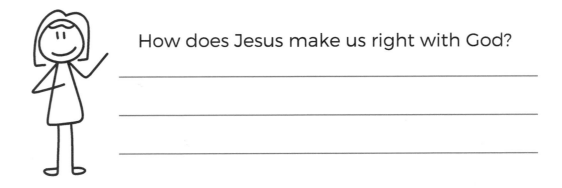

How does Jesus make us right with God?

_____

_____

_____

A cryptogram is a puzzle where each letter in a message is swapped with another letter. To solve it, try to figure out which letters stand for each other to reveal the hidden message—it's a fun code-breaking challenge!

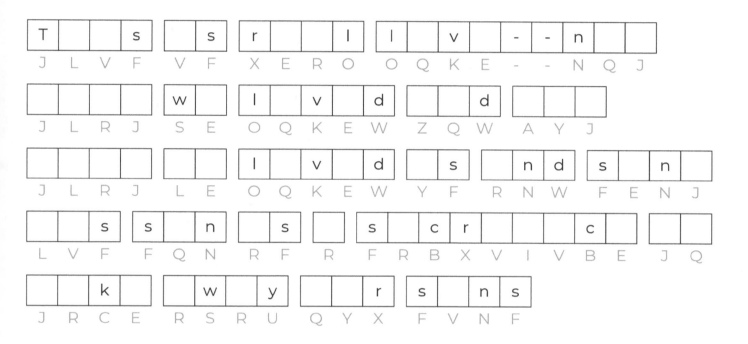

➡ For the solution, turn to 1 John 4:10 (NLT)

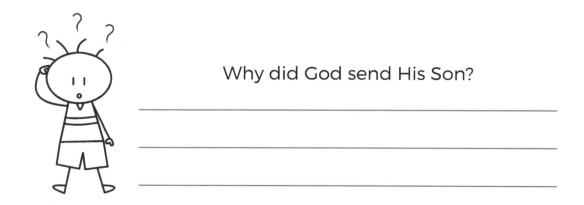

Why did God send His Son?

_____

_____

_____

Read Acts 10:36

"__This is the message of Good News__
for the people of Israel--
that __there is peace with God
through Jesus Christ,__
who is Lord of all."
Acts 10:36

What is the message
of Good News? _____

_____

Why would we need
peace with God? _____

_____

How do we get
peace with God? _____

_____

R   tions.

Read Ephesians 1:13

"And now you Gentiles have also heard the truth, the <u>Good News that God saves you</u>. And <u>when you believed in Christ, he identified you as his own by giving you the Holy Spirit</u>, whom he promised long ago."
Ephesians 1:13

What is a Gentile? _____

_____

What is the Good News?

_____

_____

What happens when we believe in Christ (Jesus)?

_____

_____

The "Good News" is that:
God wants to be close to us, so He sent JESUS CHRIST to
RESCUE US FROM the PUNISHMENT and the POWER of our sins!
Make a comic story about what this looks like to you.

GOOD NEWS WORDS

```
I  A  Q  C  Z  P  B  B  V  N  P  M  G  M  B  L
Q  J  O  H  P  E  A  C  E  K  M  E  E  L  W  F
P  Z  Q  R  G  Y  C  O  G  E  J  R  P  H  I  T
F  F  A  I  T  H  H  C  R  E  S  C  U  E  D  S
O  Y  P  S  Y  X  J  O  A  F  J  Y  O  G  A  A
R  B  Q  T  I  J  E  N  C  K  Q  M  R  T  W  L
G  O  S  P  E  L  W  F  E  J  B  Y  R  T  W  V
I  E  W  E  I  F  S  E  X  I  T  Q  E  K  D  P
V  H  B  A  P  T  I  S  M  C  R  V  P  N  Y  P
E  V  E  W  Q  J  E  S  U  S  P  P  E  Z  K  H
N  L  L  X  L  X  S  C  R  O  S  S  N  G  L  N
E  E  I  Q  C  E  G  K  F  J  M  L  T  I  A  W
S  G  E  N  T  I  L  E  S  L  S  A  V  E  D  C
S  P  V  M  G  V  S  B  E  L  I  E  V  E  Y  L
S  O  E  C  F  R  I  E  N  D  S  H  I  P  I  Y
T  S  V  E  H  L  N  K  W  Y  J  W  H  U  I  S
```

SIN	JEWS	JESUS
SAVED	GRACE	FAITH
PEACE	MERCY	CROSS
GOSPEL	REPENT	CHRIST
BELIEVE	BELIEVE	BAPTISM
RESCUED	CONFESS	GENTILES
FRIENDSHIP	FORGIVENESS	

SOLUTION

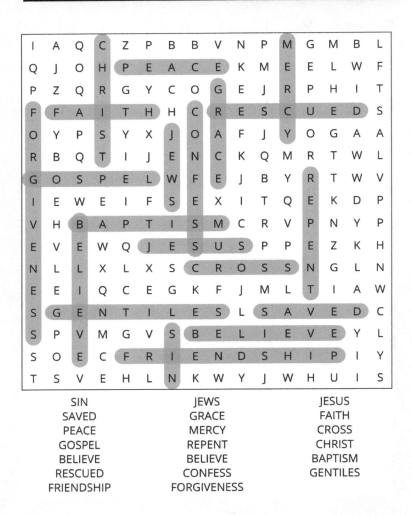

I	A	Q	C	Z	P	B	B	V	N	P	M	G	M	B	L
Q	J	O	H	P	E	A	C	E	K	M	E	E	L	W	F
P	Z	Q	R	G	Y	C	O	G	E	J	R	P	H	I	T
F	F	A	I	T	H	H	H	C	R	E	S	C	U	E	D	S
O	Y	P	S	Y	X	J	O	A	F	J	Y	O	G	A	A
R	B	Q	T	I	J	E	N	C	K	Q	M	R	T	W	L
G	O	S	P	E	L	W	F	E	J	B	Y	R	T	W	V
I	E	W	E	I	F	S	E	X	I	T	Q	E	K	D	P
V	H	B	A	P	T	I	S	M	C	R	V	P	N	Y	P
E	V	E	W	Q	J	E	S	U	S	P	P	E	Z	K	H
N	L	L	X	L	X	S	C	R	O	S	S	N	G	L	N
E	E	I	Q	C	E	G	K	F	J	M	L	T	I	A	W
S	G	E	N	T	I	L	E	S	L	S	A	V	E	D	C
S	P	V	M	G	V	S	B	E	L	I	E	V	E	Y	L
S	O	E	C	F	R	I	E	N	D	S	H	I	P	I	Y
T	S	V	E	H	L	N	K	W	Y	J	W	H	U	I	S

SIN	JEWS	JESUS
SAVED	GRACE	FAITH
PEACE	MERCY	CROSS
GOSPEL	REPENT	CHRIST
BELIEVE	BELIEVE	BAPTISM
RESCUED	CONFESS	GENTILES
FRIENDSHIP	FORGIVENESS	

18

WHAT IS THE MESSAGE OF GOOD NEWS?
DESCRIBE IT IN YOUR OWN WORDS.

GOOD NEWS

BELIEVE

Anyone who BELIEVES
and is baptized
will be saved."
Mark 16:16

WHAT DO I BELIEVE ?

TURN TO ROMANS 3 IN YOUR BIBLE AND FILL IN THE MISSING WORDS.

BELIEVE THE GOOD NEWS

GOD LOVES YOU! YOU CAN HAVE A RELATIONSHIP WITH HIM BY BELIEVING IN HIS ONE AND ONLY SON, JESUS.

ROMANS 3:22
WE ARE _____ _____ WITH GOD BY PLACING OUR _____ IN _____ _____. AND THIS IS TRUE FOR _____ WHO _____, NO MATTER WHO WE ARE."

What am I supposed to believe?

BELIEVE YOU NEED THE GOOD NEWS

ADMIT THAT YOU HAVE SINNED-- YOU HAVE TURNED FROM GOD AND CAN'T MAKE THINGS RIGHT WITH HIM ON YOUR OWN.

ROMANS 3:23
"FOR _____ HAS SINNED; WE ALL _____ _____ OF GOD'S GLORIOUS STANDARD."

BELIEVE THAT THE GOOD NEWS MAKES YOU RIGHTEOUS (INNOCENT)

GOD LOVES YOU! HE IS KIND TO YOU AND WANTS TO FORGIVE YOU. JESUS HAS TAKEN THE BLAME FOR THE WRONG YOU DO, AND MAKES IT POSSIBLE TO BE CLOSE TO GOD.

ROMANS 3:24
"YET GOD, IN HIS _____, FREELY MAKES US_____ IN HIS _____. HE DID THIS THROUGH _____ _____ WHEN HE FREED US FROM THE _____ FOR OUR SINS."

ROMANS 3:22

```
M  M  M  S  G  2  W  R  P  R  I  8  9  3
I  A  S  A  O  5  V  A  6  O  I  P  X  3
R  J  A  R  D  F  O  R  Q  M  G  G  9  R
B  4  B  L  R  E  T  P  U  A  H  O  H  L
E  S  C  Y  R  R  3  S  I  N  R  F  U  T
L  V  2  A  P  I  N  J  E  S  U  S  P  A
I  L  E  I  U  L  S  H  C  3  T  4  Y  A
E  W  Z  R  X  D  A  M  H  2  8  R  O  Z
V  P  9  Y  Y  G  I  C  R  2  6  K  U  U
E  J  9  O  M  O  F  A  I  T  H  I  S  E
S  9  H  D  H  O  N  M  S  N  V  S  T  G
X  W  Z  T  H  A  8  E  T  F  G  7  V  Z
X  3  I  5  T  T  O  8  B  U  A  B  4  W
9  W  F  B  9  O  U  R  9  1  B  L  7  5
```

WEARE	MADE	RIGHT
WITH	GOD	BYPLACING
OUR	FAITH	INJESUS
CHRIST	THIS	ISTRUE
FOR	EVERYONE	WHO
BELIEVES	ROMANS322	

SOLUTION

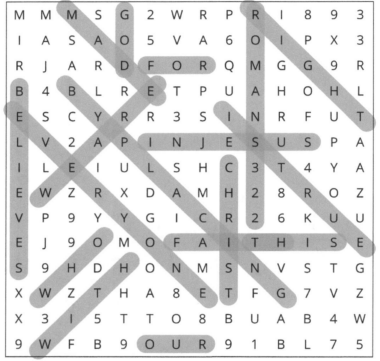

M	M	M	S	G	2	W	R	P	R	I	8	9	3
I	A	S	A	O	5	V	A	6	O	I	P	X	3
R	J	A	R	D	F	O	R	Q	M	G	G	9	R
B	4	B	L	R	E	T	P	U	A	H	O	H	L
E	S	C	Y	R	R	3	S	I	N	R	F	U	T
L	V	2	A	P	I	N	J	E	S	U	S	P	A
I	L	E	I	U	L	S	H	C	3	T	4	Y	A
E	W	Z	R	X	D	A	M	H	2	8	R	O	Z
V	P	9	Y	Y	G	I	C	R	2	6	K	U	U
E	J	9	O	M	O	F	A	I	T	H	I	S	E
S	9	H	D	H	O	N	M	S	N	V	S	T	G
X	W	Z	T	H	A	8	E	T	F	G	7	V	Z
X	3	I	5	T	T	O	8	B	U	A	B	4	W
9	W	F	B	9	O	U	R	9	1	B	L	7	5

WEARE	MADE	RIGHT
WITH	GOD	BYPLACING
OUR	FAITH	INJESUS
CHRIST	THIS	ISTRUE
FOR	EVERYONE	WHO
BELIEVES	ROMANS322	

BELIEVE

WHAT ARE SOME OTHER WORDS FOR "BELIEVE"?

UNSCRAMBLE THE FOLLOWING WORDS TO FIND OUT.

Hmm...

usttr   __ __ __ __ __

fitah   __ __ __ __ __

inthk   __ __ __ __ __   to be true

codevnnic   __ __ __ __ __ __ __ __ __

be mmcottide   __ __ __ __ __ __ __ __ __ to

READ THE FOLLOWING VERSES. WRITE WHAT GOD TELLS YOU TO BELIEVE IN THE BOX.

(PSST: It's good to read a couple verses before and after the verse listed so you understand the context.)

John 1:12

John 6:29

John 8:24

John 20:30-31

UNBELIEF

WHAT ARE **OPPOSITE** WORDS FOR "BELIEVE"?

UNSCRAMBLE THE FOLLOWING WORDS TO FIND OUT.

Hmm...

ercjet   __ __ __ __ __ __

nyde   __ __ __ __

inroge   __ __ __ __ __ __

dtsiustr   __ __ __ __ __ __ __ __

prdsoive   __ __ __ __ __ __ __ __

reject, deny, ignore, distrust, disprove

WHAT DOES IT MEAN TO
BELIEVE THE GOOD NEWS?
DESCRIBE IT IN YOUR OWN WORDS.

BELIEVE

BAPTIZED

"Anyone who believes and is BAPTIZED will be saved."
Mark 16:16

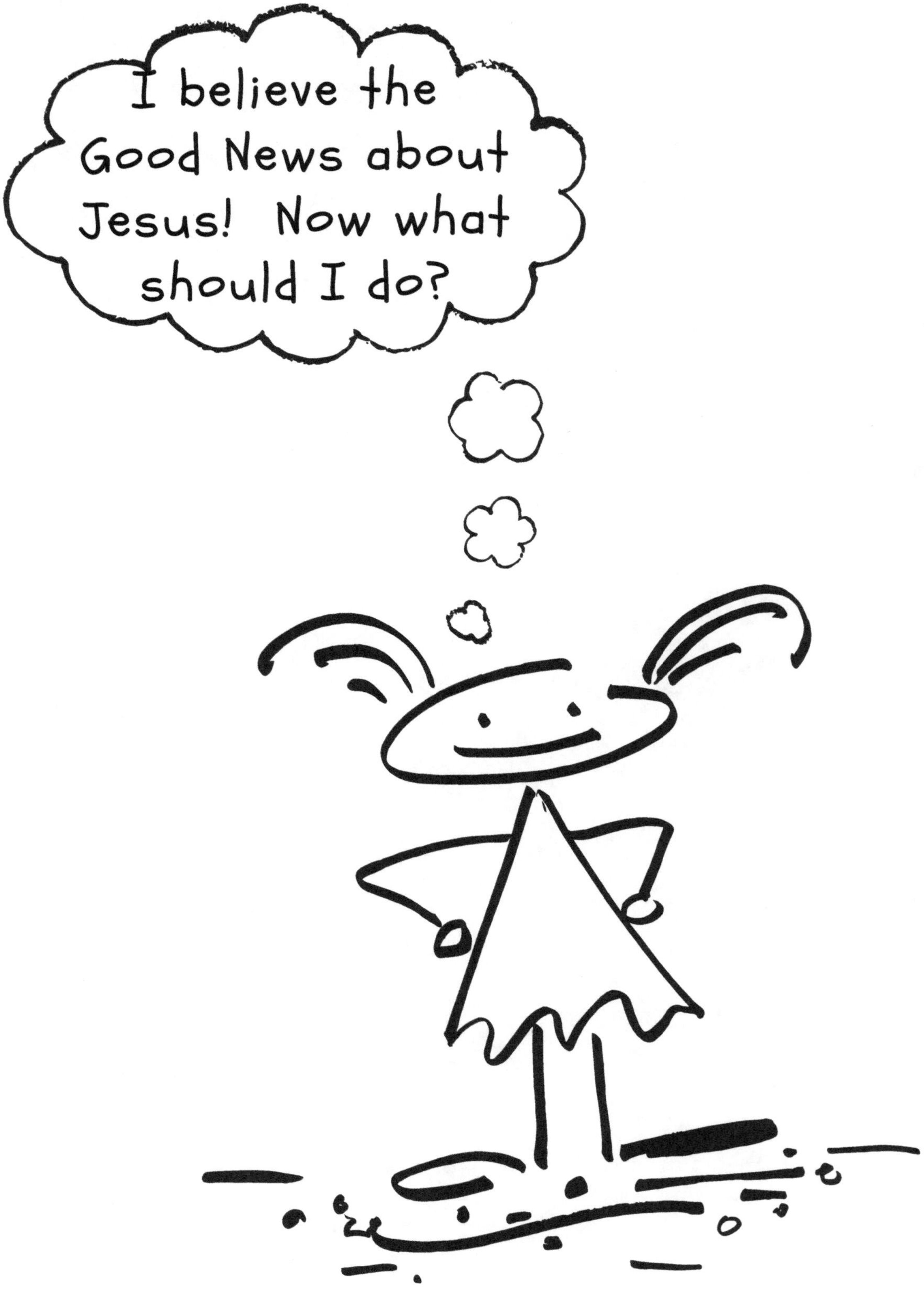
I believe the Good News about Jesus! Now what should I do?

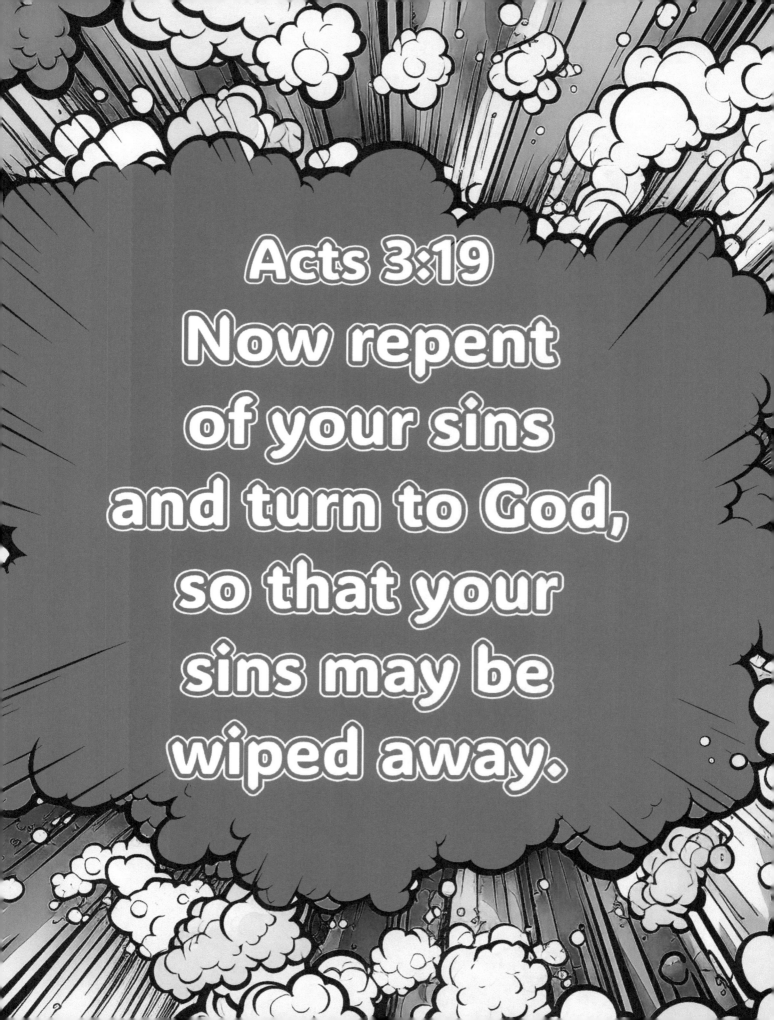

TURN TO ACTS 2:38 IN YOUR BIBLE AND FILL IN THE MISSING WORDS.

ACTS 2:38
"EACH OF YOU MUST _____ OF YOUR _____,

REPENT

SIN IS REBELLION AGAINST GOD--THINKING THAT WE KNOW BETTER THAN HIM.

SIN IS LIKE A POISON. IT MAKES YOUR HEART NOT WORK PROPERLY AND IT LEADS TO DEATH BECAUSE IT SEPARATES US FROM GOD.

WHEN WE **REPENT**, WE CHANGE OUR MIND ABOUT OUR SIN. INSTEAD OF THIKING IT'S NOT A BIG DEAL, WE HATE IT AND WANT SIN OUT OF OUR HEART.

ACTS 2:38 "_____ TO GOD,

TURN TO GOD

TURNING TO GOD MEANS TELLING HIM WHAT OUR SIN IS, AND ASKING HIM TO TAKE THE POISON OUT OF OUR HEART. WE TURN AWAY FROM OUR SIN, AND TURN TOWARD GOD.

WE CAN'T GET THE POISON OUT ON OUR OWN. BUT JESUS CAN! THAT'S THE GOOD NEWS--HE REMOVES THE ICKY SIN AND MAKES US FRIENDS WITH GOD.

ACTS 2:38
"BE _____ IN THE NAME OF _____ _____ TO SHOW THAT YOU HAVE RECEIVED _____ FOR YOUR SINS."

BE BAPTIZED

WATER BAPTISM MEANS TO BE IMMERSED IN WATER.

BEING BAPTIZED LETS OTHERS KNOW THAT YOU HAVE RECEIVED GOD'S FORGIVENESS, AND THAT YOU WANT TO FOLLOW AND OBEY JESUS.

WHAT DOES BAPTISM DO?

ROMANS 6:4A

For we _____ and were _____ with Christ by
_____.

ROMANS 6:4B

Now we also may live _____ _____.

ROMANS 6:5

Since we have been united with him in his death, we will also be
_____ _____ _____ as he was.

ROMANS 6:6A

We know that our old _____ _____ were crucified
with Christ so that _____ might lose its _____ in our lives.

ROMANS 6:6B

We are _____ _____ _____ to sin.

ROMANS 6:7

For when we _____ with _____ we were set free from
the _____ of _____.

ROMANS 6:8

And since we died with Christ, we know we will also _____
with him

34

I believe the Good News about Jesus!

START

REPENT & TURN TO GOD

FINISH

BE BAPTIZED!

(solution is on the next page)

35

Water baptism helps you follow God; giving you special power to say "no" to sin, and "yes" to God. Make a word picture from the following verse about what happens in baptism.

(example: 👁 🩶 **U** = I love you)

"We know that our old sinful selves were crucified with Christ so that sin might lose its power in our lives. We are no longer slaves to sin."
Romans 6:6

WHAT HAVE YOU LEARNED
ABOUT BAPTISM?

BAPTISM

SAVED

"Anyone who believes
and is baptized will
be SAVED."
Mark 16:16

WHAT DOES IT MEAN TO BE SAVED?

"Everyone who calls on the name of the LORD will be saved."
Romans 10:13

What does it mean to "be saved"?
Make a comic story about what
you think it looks like.

HOW ARE WE SAVED???

LOOK UP **EPHESIANS 2** IN YOUR BIBLE.
FILL IN THE MISSING WORDS:

Ephesians 2:1-5 (New Living Translation)

"Once you were dead because of your _____ and your many _____. You used to live in _____, just like the rest of the world, obeying the devil—the commander of the powers in the unseen world. He is the spirit at work in the hearts of those who _____ to obey God.

All of us used to live that way, following the passionate desires and inclinations of our sinful _____. By our very nature we were subject to God's _____, just like everyone else.

But God is so rich in _____, and he loved us so much, that even though we were dead because of our sins, he gave us life when he raised Christ from the dead. (It is only by God's _____ that you have been _____!)"

Ephesians 2:8-9 (New Living Translation)

"God _____ you by his _____ when you believed. And you can't take credit for this; it is a _____ from God.

Salvation is _____ a _____ for the good things we have done, so none of us can boast about it."

only by

GOD'S

GRACE

have I been

SAVED!

45

SAVED

WHAT ARE SOME OTHER WORDS FOR "SAVED"?

UNSCRAMBLE THE FOLLOWING WORDS TO FIND OUT.

HMM...

esruce __ __ __ __ __ __ from danger

egt aywa __ __ __   __ __ __ __

aeescp __ __ __ __ __ __

hlae __ __ __ __

rersteo __ __ __ __ __ __ __

BAM!

rescue, get away, escape, heal, restore

47

WHAT ARE WE SAVED FROM ??

Connect what JESUS SAVES US FROM by drawing a line to the correct Bible verse.

OUR SIN	Romans 6:23
GOD'S ANGER	Matthew 1:21
DEATH	Romans 2:5-8
DESTRUCTION	Hebrews 10:39

WHY ARE WE SAVED???

Connect the reason JESUS SAVES US by drawing a line to the correct Bible verse.

LIVE FOREVER WITH GOD	Titus 3:4-5
FRIENDSHIP	John 1:12
CHILD OF GOD	Romans 5:9-11
GOOD WORKS	1 Thessalonians 5:9-10
GOD'S MERCY	Ephesians 2:8-10

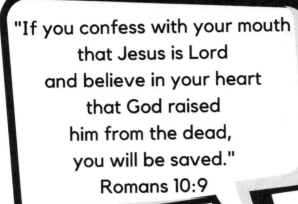

"If you confess with your mouth that Jesus is Lord and believe in your heart that God raised him from the dead, you will be saved."
Romans 10:9

"For it is by believing in your heart that you are made right with God, and it is by confessing with your mouth that you are saved."
Romans 10:10

WHAT DOES IT MEAN TO BE "SAVED"? DESCRIBE IT IN YOUR OWN WORDS.

SAVED

CONDEMNED

"But anyone who REFUSES to believe will be CONDEMNED."
Mark 16:16

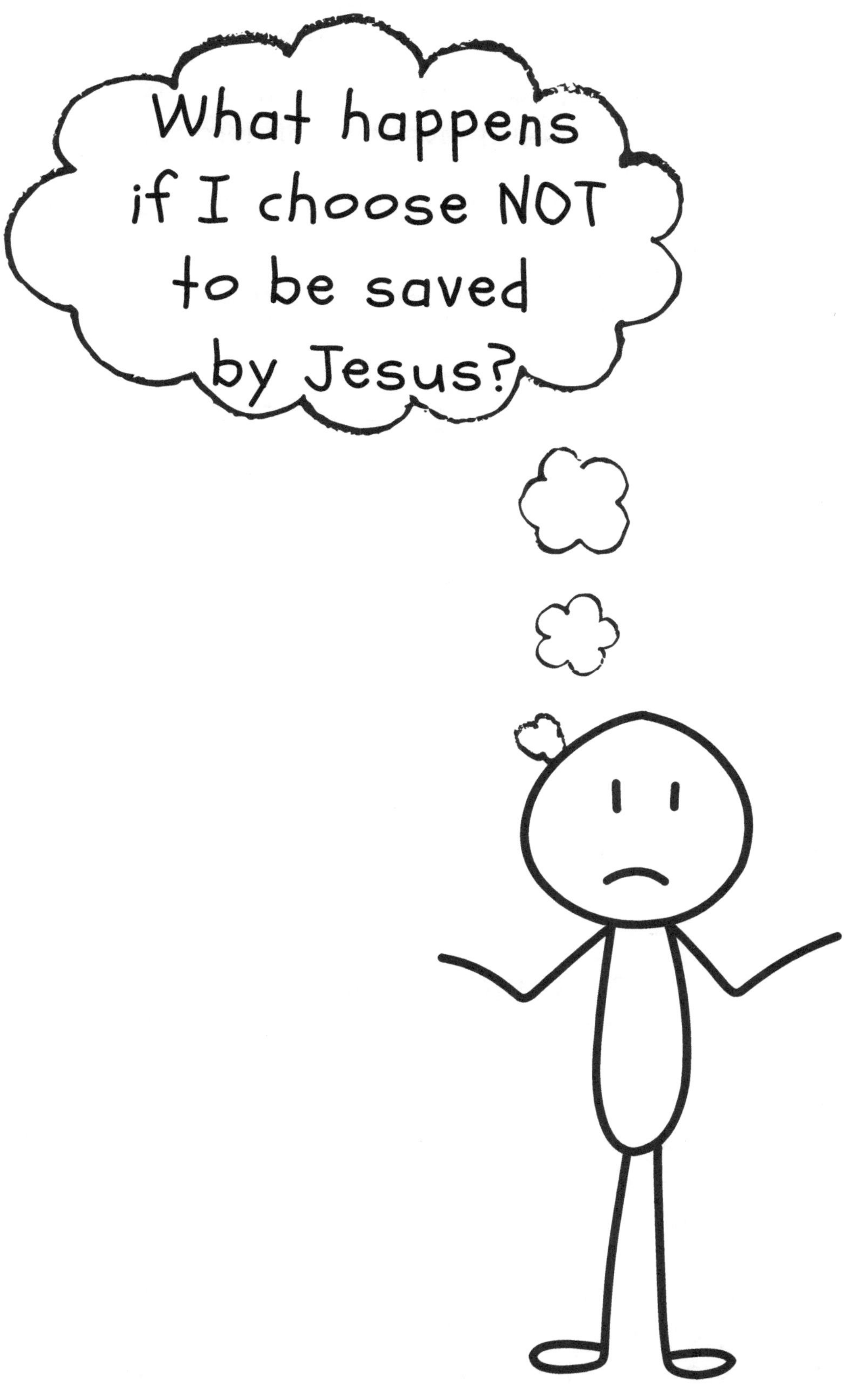
What happens if I choose NOT to be saved by Jesus?

Condemnation is not very fun to talk about. But, in order to be grateful for the Good News, we need to know the bad news.

Everybody has 2 options to choose from:
salvation (being saved) or condemnation.

What does it mean to be condemned?

To be condemned means:

DOOMED
CURSED
DECLARED GUILTY
SENTENCED TO DIE
basically...
SPEND FOREVER IN HELL
APART FROM GOD

That is REALLY bad news!
And that's why the Good News is soooooo good.

If we turn to God's Son, Jesus...if we believe we are sinners and need someone to rescue us from being condemned...then God gives us the gift of salvation--ETERNAL LIFE! We become His child, and we never need to fear death or hell.

However, if we ignore Jesus...if we think we can be a good enough person...if we think our sin is not that big of a deal...then we are rejecting God and we are choosing death.

Make a "word picture" from the following verse.
(example: 👁 🖤 U = I love you)

JESUS SAID:
"The world's sin is that it refuses to believe in me."
John 16:9

READ THE VERSE AND ANSWER THE QUESTIONS

Read Romans 10:3

"For they don't understand God's way of making people right with himself.

Refusing to accept God's way,

they cling to their own way of getting right with God by trying to keep the law.

What do people not understand?_____

_____

What are the people clinging to?_____

_____

Have you ever thought, or heard someone say, that *I am going to heaven because I'm a "good person"*. Well, that's believing you are going to get right with God by "keeping the law". When a person believes that way, they are refusing to accept God's way.

READ THE VERSE AND ANSWER THE QUESTIONS

Read Romans 10:4

"For Christ has already accomplished the purpose for which the law was given.

As a result, all who believe in him are made right with God."

What has Jesus Christ accomplished?_____

_____

What is the result of Jesus perfectly keeping all the rules (Law) for us (because we are unable)?

_____

_____

No one can come to Father God except through Jesus (John 14:6). Trusting in Jesus, not being a "good person," is the ONLY way to be made right with God, and receive eternal life.

SOLVE THIS CRYPTOGRAM

A cryptogram is a puzzle where each letter in a message is swapped with another letter. To solve it, try to figure out which letters stand for each other to reveal the hidden message—it's a fun code-breaking challenge!

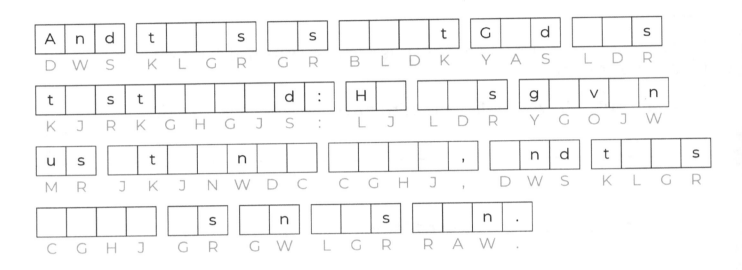

For the solution, turn to 1 John 5:11 (NLT)

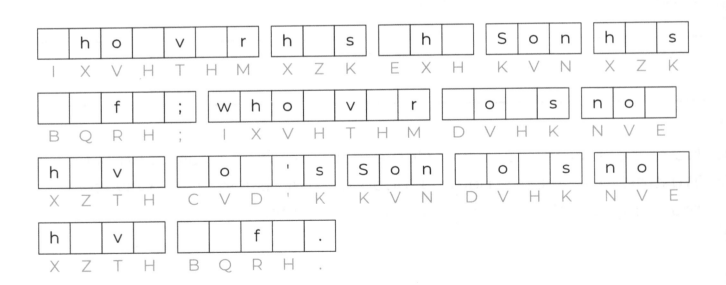

For the solution, turn to 1 John 5:12 (NLT)

GOD LOVES YOU SO MUCH, SO HE MADE A WAY TO ADOPT YOU AS HIS CHILD. HE OFFERS YOU THIS RELATIONSHIP AS A GIFT. YOU RECEIVE HIS GIFT BY BELIEVING IN JESUS AND TRUSTING HIM TO SAVE YOU.

THERE IS NO WAY YOU CAN BE GOOD ENOUGH TO EARN YOUR WAY TO HEAVEN. THOSE WHO REFUSE TO TRUST IN JESUS ARE REFUSING GOD'S GIFT THAT HE OFFERS TO ALL OF US.

Ephesians 2:8-9

God saved you by his _____ when you _____. And you can't take credit for this; it is a _____ from God. Salvation is _____ a

_____ for the good things we have done, so _____ of us can boast about it."

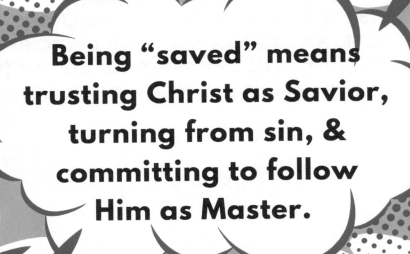

Being "saved" means trusting Christ as Savior, turning from sin, & committing to follow Him as Master.

SALVATION   OR   CONDEMNATION

SALVATION	CONDEMNATION
ETERNAL LIFE	ETERNAL DEATH
FORGIVENESS OF SINS	JUDGEMENT OF SINS
FREEDOM FROM SIN'S POWER	SLAVE TO SIN'S POWER
FRIENDSHIP WITH GOD	ENEMIES WITH GOD
JESUS TAKING THE PUNISHMENT FOR MY SINS	ME TAKING THE PUNISHMENT FOR MY SINS
DOING THINGS GOD'S WAY	DOING THINGS MY OWN WAY
RIGHTEOUSNESS (GOD SEEING ME WITH NO FAULTS)	SINFULNESS (GOD SEEING ALL MY FAULTS)
PEACE	FEAR

WHAT IS THE DIFFERENCE BETWEEN BEING SAVED VS. BEING CONDEMNED?

SAVED OR CONDEMNED

GO... AND PREACH

"GO into all the world and PREACH the Good News to everyone."
Mark 16:16

VERSE 13:

EVERYONE WHO _____ ON THE NAME OF THE _____ WILL BE _____."

People need to HEAR about JESUS

VERSE 14:

BUT HOW CAN THEY CALL ON HIM TO _____ THEM UNLESS THEY _____ IN HIM? AND HOW CAN THEY BELIEVE IN HIM IF THEY HAVE NEVER _____ ABOUT HIM? AND HOW CAN THEY _____ ABOUT HIM UNLESS _____ TELLS THEM?

WHO CAN YOU TELL THE GOOD NEWS TO?

God loves the people He created! He wants us to tell them the Good News that He loves them and wants to be close to them. But when we tell them, He wants us to have love in our hearts.

I Cor. 13:1
If I could speak all the languages of earth and of angels, but didn't love others, I would only be a noisy gong or a clanging cymbal.

Make 1 comic about telling others the Good News WITHOUT love....

...and 1 comic about telling others the Good News WITH love....

Read 1 Cor. 13:4-7 to learn what love is

Now that you know the Good News,
God wants you to share it!

God loves everyone and wants them to hear
about Jesus and how to be close to Him.

We can't save our friends or family—only Jesus
can do that. But we can pray for them!

Who can you pray for that needs to hear the Good News?

2 PETER 3:9

S	I	K	I	L	H	P	D	O	E	S	N	O	T
S	D	M	E	W	L	D	F	X	V	K	K	M	Y
C	N	E	H	A	S	W	A	X	E	E	V	B	P
V	F	Y	S	N	J	H	T	N	R	S	I	V	Q
K	H	K	L	T	Z	L	X	V	Y	X	P	C	F
Z	I	D	X	S	R	K	A	T	O	O	V	N	M
D	P	I	T	B	G	O	D	O	N	Q	N	B	Z
X	Z	Q	W	J	V	M	Y	R	E	V	Y	E	Q
U	A	A	B	U	T	I	I	E	I	W	E	E	I
M	E	E	D	F	E	K	A	P	D	W	E	Y	E
B	R	V	S	S	T	J	H	E	X	A	F	B	C
U	Q	A	K	J	H	I	S	N	I	N	O	O	H
A	Z	A	F	L	C	L	I	T	R	T	E	G	G
G	J	G	M	Q	L	X	C	K	C	N	U	P	Y

GOD
ANYONE
BUT
TO REPENT

DOES NOT
TO BE
WANTS

WANT
DESTROYED
EVERYONE

SOLUTION

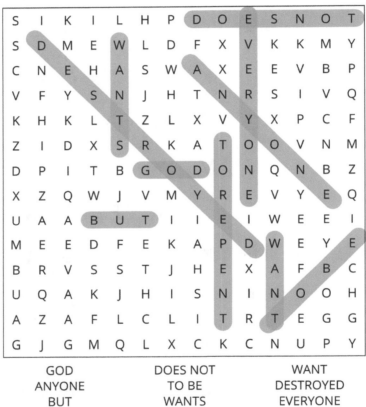

S	I	K	I	L	H	P	D	O	E	S	N	O	T
S	D	M	E	W	L	D	F	X	V	K	K	M	Y
C	N	E	H	A	S	W	A	X	E	E	V	B	P
V	F	Y	S	N	J	H	T	N	R	S	I	V	Q
K	H	K	L	T	Z	L	X	V	Y	X	P	C	F
Z	I	D	X	S	R	K	A	T	O	O	V	N	M
D	P	I	T	B	G	O	D	O	N	Q	N	B	Z
X	Z	Q	W	J	V	M	Y	R	E	V	Y	E	Q
U	A	A	B	U	T	I	I	E	I	W	E	E	I
M	E	E	D	F	E	K	A	P	D	W	E	Y	E
B	R	V	S	S	T	J	H	E	X	A	F	B	C
U	Q	A	K	J	H	I	S	N	I	N	O	O	H
A	Z	A	F	L	C	L	I	T	R	T	E	G	G
G	J	G	M	Q	L	X	C	K	C	N	U	P	Y

GOD	DOES NOT	WANT
ANYONE	TO BE	DESTROYED
BUT	WANTS	EVERYONE
TO REPENT		

RESPOND

Jesus asked him:
"But who do you
say I am?"
Mark 8:29

I believe:

Name: _____   Date: _____

Read the following statements, and mark whether you agree or not.

	Yes	No
I believe God loves me	☐	☐
I believe I am a sinner	☐	☐
I believe that sin is like poison in my heart	☐	☐
I believe that if I'm good enough, I will go to heaven	☐	☐
I believe Jesus is God's Son, and that He died to take the poison of sin out of my life	☐	☐
I believe Jesus makes me innocent if I ask Him to, and that gives me peace with God	☐	☐
I believe water baptism lets others know that I accept God's forgiveness	☐	☐
I believe water baptism gives me special power from God to say "no" to sin	☐	☐
I believe that it doesn't really matter if I ignore Jesus	☐	☐
I have personally asked Jesus to forgive my sins and I want to obey Him	☐	☐
I believe that I am God's child, and He pays special attention to me	☐	☐

Write A Prayer to Jesus

_____
_____
_____
_____
_____
_____
_____
_____
_____
_____
_____
_____
_____
_____
_____
_____
_____
_____
_____
_____
_____
_____

Thank Jesus for saving you by taking the punishment for the wrong things you've done.

If you've never asked Him to forgive you and make you friends with God—but you want to—you can ask Him right now!

Good job finishing this Digging Into God Activity Book! Now that you have learned the Good News about Jesus, and that God wants to be close to you and has made a way for that to be possible--keep getting closer and becoming better friends with Him!

Here are a few ways you can grow closer to God:
reading your Bible to discover more about Him (the Bible is God's main way of talking to you!),

talking to the Lord as you go about your day (Tell your Heavenly Father about what you are enjoying, things you need help with, how you are feeling, etc.),

trusting that God is always with you (when you play sports, when you take a test at school, when you sleep),

obeying what He says and trusting that God's way is what is BEST for you (and asking for help when it is hard--ie: being kind to your sister when she has been mean to you).

If you need a tool to help you develop the habit of spending time with the Lord each day, check out **diggingintoGod.com**.

"Go into all the world and preach the Good News to everyone. Anyone who believes and is baptized will be saved. But anyone who refuses to believe will be condemned."

If you need tools to help you and your family grow in their relationship with the Lord, go to **diggingintoGod.com.**

You will find Bible studies for kids, teens, and adults; Christian education resources; Bible verse handwriting books; prayer notebooks; and much more!

Made in United States
Troutdale, OR
02/06/2025

28706494R00044